THIS WALKER BOOK BELONGS TO:

_____

_____

_____

_____

"I have a little shadow
that goes in and out with me..."
For Marmers
P. D.

First published 1999 by Walker Books Ltd
87 Vauxhall Walk, London SE11 5HJ

This edition published 2001

2 4 6 8 10 9 7 5 3 1

Illustrations © 1999 Penny Dale

This book has been typeset in Stempel Schneidler

Printed in Hong Kong

British Library Cataloguing in Publication Data:
a catalogue record for this book
is available from the British Library

ISBN 0-7445-8299-7

My Shadow

ROBERT LOUIS STEVENSON

illustrated by **PENNY DALE**

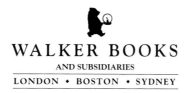

WALKER BOOKS
AND SUBSIDIARIES

LONDON • BOSTON • SYDNEY

I have a little shadow
   that goes in and out with me,

And what can be the use of him
is more than I can see.

He is very, very like me
   from the heels up to the head;

And I see him jump before me,
when I jump into my bed.

The funniest thing about him
is the way he likes to grow –

Not at all like proper children,
which is always very slow;

For he sometimes shoots up taller
like an india-rubber ball,

And he sometimes gets so little
that there's none of him at all.

He hasn't got a notion of
how children ought to play,

And can only make a fool of me
in every sort of way.

He stays so close beside me,
he's a coward you can see;

I'd think shame to stick to nursie
as that shadow sticks to me!

One morning, very early,
before the sun was up,

I rose and found the shining dew
on every buttercup;

But my lazy little shadow,
like an arrant sleepy-head,

Had stayed at home behind me
and was fast asleep in bed.

ROBERT LOUIS STEVENSON (1850–1894) grew up in Edinburgh. Though his parents wanted him to be a lighthouse engineer and then a lawyer, he always knew he wanted to write. Many of his stories and poems have since become classics, such as *Treasure Island, Kidnapped* and *The Strange Case of Dr Jekyll and Mr Hyde*. **My Shadow** is taken from the collection of poems *A Child's Garden of Verses*, which is based on memories of the poet's own childhood.

PENNY DALE says of *My Shadow*, "When I was a child, my favourite shadow was the long, thin, elastic one that came to copy me when the sun was low. This poem captures the curiosity and playfulness of childhood, and gave me an opportunity to play with shadows all over again."

Penny Dale is one of this country's leading illustrators of children's books. Her first book was published in 1986 and she has since written and illustrated many, many more, including *Wake Up, Mr B!* (Commended for the Kate Greenaway Medal); *Big Brother, Little Brother; Ten in the Bed; Ten Out of Bed* and *Ten Play Hide-and-Seek*. She has also illustrated several stories by the author Martin Waddell: *Once There Were Giants, When the Teddy Bears Came, Rosie's Babies* (Winner of the Best Books for Babies Award) and *Night Night, Cuddly Bear*. Penny lives in Wales with her family.